# Healthy and Cheap Dog Treats to Spoil Your Pup

## Prepare Easy Dog Treats with These Recipes

### BY: Nancy Silverman

# COPYRIGHT NOTICES

© 2021 Nancy Silverman All Rights Reserved

Subject to the agreement and permission of the author, this Book, in part or in whole, may not be reproduced in any format. This includes but is not limited to electronically, in print, scanning or photocopying.

The opinions, guidelines and suggestions written here are solely those of the Author and are for information purposes only. Every possible measure has been taken by the Author to ensure accuracy but let the Reader be advised that they assume all risk when following information. The Author does not assume any risk in the case of damages, personally or commercially, in the case of misinterpretation or misunderstanding while following any part of the Book.

# Table of Contents

Introduction ................................................................................................ 6

    Pumpkin peanut butter dog treats ........................................................... 8

    Banana oatmeal dog treats .................................................................... 10

    Banana and yogurt dog treats ................................................................ 12

    Tuna biscuit dog treats .......................................................................... 14

    Blueberry cookie dog treats ................................................................... 16

    Apple cinnamon dog treats .................................................................... 18

    Cheese dog treats ................................................................................. 20

    Healthy sweet potato fries dog treats .................................................... 22

    Icy apple dog treats .............................................................................. 24

    Heart-shaped dog treats ....................................................................... 26

    Cranberry cookie dog treats .................................................................. 28

    Salmon brownies for pups .................................................................... 30

    Valentine dog treats ............................................................................. 32

    Pumpkin cupcakes ............................................................................... 34

Zucchini dog treats ............................................................................................. 37

Icy watermelon doggy popsicles ....................................................................... 39

Strawberry banana dog treats ............................................................................ 41

Chicken biscuits ................................................................................................ 43

Triple cheese dog biscuits ................................................................................. 45

Special icing for dog cookies ............................................................................ 47

Heart shaped cookie sandwiches for pups ........................................................ 49

Dog treats for fresh breath ................................................................................ 52

Simple dog treats .............................................................................................. 54

Puppy donuts .................................................................................................... 56

Herbs dog treats ................................................................................................ 58

Pumpkin dog ice cream .................................................................................... 60

Bacon bites ....................................................................................................... 62

Puppy breath treats ........................................................................................... 64

Blackberry cheesecake dog treats ..................................................................... 66

Puppy pancakes ................................................................................................ 68

Conclusion ............................................................................................................ 70

About the Author .................................................................................................. 71

Author's Afterthoughts ......................................................................................... 72

# Introduction

There are so many reasons why you should start preparing homemade doggie treats. The first one is your pet's health. Dogs do experience health problems as a result of poor diet, so make healthy choices for them. When you prepare the treats contained in this Dog Treat Recipes cookbook, you will see that there is a limited choice of ingredients suitable for dogs.

Next comes the money. We know that having a pet can be costly, so reduce your costs by preparing homemade treats. This Dog Treat Recipes cookbook has all you need to get started. No need to search for vet-approved ingredients and to come up with the right combination. We packed everything here for your convenience.

Are you ready to get started? Let's hop onto the first recipe and get going! Your dog will be so thankful.

# Pumpkin peanut butter dog treats

Peanut butter is an excellent ingredient for puppies. However, you need to make sure that you get a xylitol free version. This is an artificial sweetener that isn't recommended for dogs. You are free to use regular peanut butter and prepare a sweet treat for your precious pup.

**Cooking time: 2 hours**

**Yields:30**

**Ingredients:**

- 1/4 Cup Peanut Butter
- 8oz Can Pureed Pumpkin, no additives
- 1/4 Cup Coconut Oil
- 2 Teaspoons Cinnamon

**Instructions:**

Place all of the pup treats ingredients in a food processor or blender.

Pulse until they are completely mixed. Make sure that the pureed pumpkin doesn't contain any artificial sweeteners or additives.

Pour into silicone paw molds. Freeze for at least 2 hours and let your pup enjoy the tasty treat.

# Banana oatmeal dog treats

While you enjoy oatmeal and banana, keep in mind that this is a good combo for pups as well. You will love to see their tails wiggle while they ask for one more piece.

**Cooking time:30 minutes**

**Yields:12**

**Ingredients:**

- 1 egg
- 1 cup whole wheat flour
- 1/3 cup peanut butter
- 1/2 cup banana, mashed
- 1/2 cup oats
- 1 tablespoon coconut oil

**Instructions:**

Preheat the oven to 300.

Add the dog treat ingredients into a mixing bowl.

Mix with your hands and knead the dough. If the dough is too sticky, add some more flour.

Press it flat into a surface and use a paw or bone cookie cutter to shape the treas.

Line a baking sheet with paper and grease it with coconut oil.

Bake for 20 minutes and cool down before serving to your puppy.

# Banana and yogurt dog treats

This makes a refreshing and tasty treat for dogs of any breed. Prepare this impel and easy recipe and let your pup enjoy the taste and nutrients.

**Cooking time:3 hours**

**Yields:50**

**Ingredients:**

- 16 oz Greek yogurt, plain version with no additives
- 1 1/2 tablespoons almond butter, unsweetened
- 1 banana

**Instructions:**

Set the silicone molds onto a flat surface such as a baking pan.

Add the treat ingredients to a blender and puree until smooth.

Fill the molds with the batter.

Store in the freezer for about 3 hours. Gently pop the treats out and serve.

# Tuna biscuit dog treats

Giving up the store-bought dog treats is easy when you have this recipe in your hands. In no time, you will whip up these tuna cookies. They are healthy and quick, so don't hesitate to head to the kitchen right now.

**Cooking time:30 minutes**

**Yields:15**

**Ingredients:**

- 2 eggs
- 2 cans of 5oz Tuna
- 1/4 cup parmesan cheese
- 1 1/2 cups of flour
- 1 tablespoon coconut oil

**Instructions:**

Preheat the oven to 350 degrees.

Add all of the ingredients in a bowl and mix.

Brush a baking pan with coconut oil and transfer the mixture.

Bake for around 25 minutes. Let it cool down before cutting.

# Blueberry cookie dog treats

If you enjoy the excellent old cookies, now it is time for your dog to do too. This simple recipe shows you how to make blueberry cookies rich in nutrients.

**Cooking time: 50 minutes**

**Yields: 35**

**Ingredients:**

- 1 cup blueberries
- ¾ cup oats
- 2 eggs
- ½ tsp salt
- 3 tbsp peanut butter
- 2 ½ cup whole wheat flour
- ½ tsp ground cinnamon
- ⅛ - ½ cup warm water

**Instructions:**

Preheat the oven to 350 degrees.

Roughly chop the blueberries.

Add The blueberries to a mixing bowl.

Add the oats and mash them together.

Add the rest of the ingredients and start with ⅛ cup water. Mix until the dough is combined.

If the dough is dry, add some more warm water.

Sprinkle flour into a flat kneading surface. Roll the dough to ½ inch thick and use cookie cutters to form the cookies.

Place on a paper-lined sheet and bake for 40 minutes.

# Apple cinnamon dog treats

Apple is on the list of vet-approved dog foods, so this is a good recipe. The apple cinnamon dog traits are perfect for the cold fall days. You will be tempted by the aroma that spreads across the kitchen, and you'd want to steal a bite.

**Cooking time: 30 minutes**

**Yields:6**

**Ingredients:**

- 1 cup Dry Quick Cook Oatmeal
- 1 large Egg
- ½ cup Cinnamon Applesauce
- 1 tablespoon olive oil

**Instructions:**

Preheat the oven to 350 degrees.

Mix the applesauce and oatmeal.

Combine the egg into the mixture.

Grease a paper-lined cookie sheet

Scoop out the mixture onto the sheet and shape the cookie.

Bake for 22 minutes and let them cool off slightly before removing.

# Cheese dog treats

How about chewy, cheesy bites for pups? This recipe includes creamy cheddar, perfect for your furry friend. Give them the treat that they deserve for being a good boy.

**Cooking time:40 minutes**

**Yields:35**

**Ingredients:**

- 2 cups of shredded cheddar cheese
- 4 cups of flour
- 1 1/3 cups of water
- 2 tbsp-1/4 cup of oil

**Instructions:**

Preheat the oven to 300 degrees. Combine the cheese and flour in a bowl.

Add in water and oil. Mix well to combine.

Sprinkle the surface with flour and roll the dough until ½ inch thick. Cut off the cookies using your favorite cookie cutter shape.

Place them on a paper-lined cookie sheet. Cook for about 20 minutes or until dry and set.

# Healthy sweet potato fries dog treats

Just because they are pups, it doesn't have to mean that I shouldn't enjoy fries. This recipe will teach you how to make healthy and dog-approved fries. You would want to enjoy some with your furry friend.

**Cooking time: 40 minutes**

**Yields:4 portions**

**Ingredients:**

- 1 tbsp Coconut Oil
- 1 Sweet Potato
- ½ teaspoon Turmeric
- ½ teaspoon Cinnamon

**Instructions:**

Preheat the oven to 425 degrees.

Peel the potato and cut it into sticks.

Add into a large bowl and sprinkle with oil and species.

Mix to cover the fries evenly.

Place the dog fries on a baking sheet and bake for 15 minutes.

Remove, flip them, and bake for an additional 15 minutes.

# Icy apple dog treats

Whenever the weather is scorching hot, the recipe will offer a referencing treat for your pups. The frozen apple treats are perfect for dogs of any breed, but especially those that can't stand the hot weather.

**Cooking time:3 hours**

**Yields:20**

**Ingredients:**

- 2 Apples
- Water, as needed
- 1 Cup Greek Nonfat Plain Yogurt

**Instructions:**

Peel the apple and remove the seeds. Cut into small chunks.

Add the apple chunks into the blender, together with the rest of the ingredients. Add just ⅛ cup water, and adjust to the desired consistency.

Blend until smooth. Pour the treat mixture into silicone molds of your choice.

Freeze for 3 hours or until hardener. Remove gently from the mold and serve.

# Heart-shaped dog treats

Give your dog the love it deserved with these lovely heart cookies. Once they try this, they will ask for one more. Don't worry because all of the ingredients are vet-approved and safe for pups.

**Cooking time:35 minutes**

**Yields:20**

**Ingredients:**

- 1/2 cup rice, cooked
- 1 cup chicken, cooked and finely chopped
- 3 tablespoons rice flour
- 1 egg
- 1 tablespoon parsley

**Instructions:**

Preheat the oven to 350 degrees.

Place the cooked rice in a mixing bowl and mash with a fork.

Add the rest of the ingredients and mix well until combined.

Transfer into silence baking molds and bake for around 25 minutes, or until golden brown.

Leave them to cool slightly and remove them from molds.

# Cranberry cookie dog treats

This recipe is so simple and easy to make that you can hit it up in no time. Your pup will be amazed, so make a double batch.

**Cooking time:30 minutes**

**Yields:15**

**Ingredients:**

- 2 Eggs
- 1 Tablespoon Coconut Oil
- 5 Cups Almond Flour
- 1/2 Cup Dried Cranberries
- 3-4 Tablespoons Coconut Flour

**Instructions:**

Preheat the oven to 325 degrees.

Beat two eggs and set them aside.

In another bowl, combine the coconut oil, almond flour, and cranberries.

Sprinkle coconut flour one tablespoon at a time until the mixture isn't sticky. Mix between adding each. It will take three or four tablespoons.

Roll the dough onto a flat surface and cut the cookies with a cookie cutter.

Place on a paper-lined baking sheet and bake for 15 minutes or until dry.

# Salmon brownies for pups

This is a versatile treat for all the good boys out there, waiting for their reward. Salmon has plenty of protein and fats, making it the right choice for your pup.

**Cooking time:1 hour 30 minutes**

**Yields:12**

**Ingredients:**

- 1 can salmon
- 2 large eggs
- 1 sweet potato, baked
- 1/3 cup coconut flour
- coconut oil, as needed

**Instructions:**

Preheat the oven to 350 degrees.

In a mixing bowl, beat the eggs.

Add salmon and coconut flour and mix to combine.

Leave the mixture to rest aside for 10 minutes.

Peel the potato and mash it, before adding to the mix.

Grease a baking pan with coconut oil and transfer the brownie mixture.

Bake for an hour or until the edges are set. Let it cool before cutting into a square shape.

# Valentine dog treats

While Valentine's day is for showing love, don't forget to appreciate your pup. Give them the love they deserve by cooking this simple and easy recipe. The cookies look so adorable and decorative.

**Cooking time:3 hours**

**Yields:15**

**Ingredients:**

- 1 cup strawberries
- 1/2 cup plain Greek yogurt
- 1 banana

**Instructions:**

Cut the banana into chunks and add it into a blender.

Add in the remaining ingredients and puree until smooth.

Pour the mix into a heart-shaped silicone mold.

Freeze for about three hours or until hardened. Gently pop the treats out and hand one or two to your pup.

# Pumpkin cupcakes

Cupcakes are an excellent choice for special occasions. Consider celebrating their birthday with these tasty cupcakes. All of the ingredients are adjusted for dogs, so feel free to treat them with a decadent and delicious dessert.

**Cooking time:40 minutes**

**Yields:6**

**Ingredients:**

*Pupcake:*

- 1 teaspoon baking powder
- 1 tablespoon maple syrup
- 1 egg, room temperature
- ½ cup whole grain oat flour
- ½ teaspoon cinnamon
- 1 tablespoon peanut butter
- ½ cup pumpkin puree
- ½ cup shredded carrot
- ¼ cup Greek yogurt

*Frosting recipe:*

- ½ tablespoon maple syrup
- ½ cup Greek yogurt
- 1/4 cup peanut butter

**Instructions:**

Preheat the oven to 350 degrees.

Add all of the pupcake ingredients into a large mixing bowl. Mix well to combine.

Grease a muffin tin with six compartments and pour the mixture.

Bake for 35 minutes or until dry. Leave them to cool down thoroughly before continuing with the frosting

Add all of the ingredients into a mixing bowl and mix to combine.

Transfer into a piping bag and decorate your pupcakes.

# Zucchini dog treats

Veggies are healthy for pups, so consider this zucchini dog treat recipe. Despite being too quick and straightforward to make, it will become their favorite treat. A simple and delicious treat that they will want to munch on.

**Cooking time:50 Minutes**

**Yields:35**

**Ingredients:**

- 1 cup pumpkin puree
- 2 eggs
- 1/4 cup peanut butter
- 3 cups whole wheat flour
- 1/2 cup rolled oats
- 1 medium carrot, shredded
- 1 cup spinach, chopped
- 1 medium zucchini, shredded

**Instructions:**

Preheat your oven to 350 degrees.

Beat the eggs, puree, and peanut butter with a mixer for two minutes.

Add 2 ½ cups flour and the oats gradually into the mixture while still beating on low.

Continue to add the rest of the flour if the mixture is too sticky.

Add the veggies and beat to incorporate them into the dough.

Roll onto a flat surface until ¼ inch thick. Cut with a cookie cutter into the desired shapes.

Line the baking sheet with paper and place the cookies. Bake for 25 minutes or until crisp.

# Icy watermelon doggy popsicles

This is another great summer recipe for your pup. The icy watermelon popsicles are an excellent option for the hot summer days. Let your dog enjoy the sweet and refreshing flavor, and have them ready in your freezer any time.

**Cooking time:3 hours**

**Yields:30**

**Ingredients:**

- 2 cups of seedless watermelon
- 1 tablespoon of honey
- 1 cup of coconut milk

**Instructions:**

Scoop out the watermelon and cut it into chunks.

Place in the blender and blend until smooth.

Add the honey and coconut milk. Blend again to combine.

Pour into the desired silicone molds and freeze for around three hours or until hardened.

# Strawberry banana dog treats

This sweet doggy snack is a must. Don't forget to prepare a double batch because your pup will love the flavor.

**Cooking time:15minutes**

**Yields:35**

**Ingredients:**

- 1 egg
- 1/3 cup peanut butter
- 1 cup Wheat flour
- 1/2 cup oats
- 1/2 cup banana mashed
- 5 strawberries finely chopped

**Instructions:**

Preheat the oven to 300 degrees.

Add the ingredients into a mixing bowl. Mix well and knead the dough with your hands. If it appears to be sticky, add a little bit more flour.

Add some flour on a flat surface and roll the dog treat dough. Use cookie cutters to cut out the treats and place them onto a baking sheet lined with parchment paper.

Bike for 25 minutes and let them cool before removing.

# Chicken biscuits

These biscuits are a great treat for our pup. They contain natural ingredients, so you don't have to worry about nutrition. All you need to do is head to the kitchen because you likely have all the ingredients there.

**Cooking time: 40 minutes**

**Yields: 24**

**Ingredients:**

- 2 1/2 cups wheat flour
- 1 egg
- 1 chicken bouillon cube
- 1/2 cup water
- 2 tablespoons parsley chopped
- 1 tsp salt

**Instructions:**

Heat the oven to 350 degrees.

Mix the water and bouillon in a pot and heat on the stove until dissolved.

Pour it into a bowl together with the rest of the ingredients.

Cover the cookie cutter in flour and cut out the shapes.

Place on a sheet lined with baking paper and bake for 30 minutes. Allow to cool before removing.

# Triple cheese dog biscuits

A triple cheese biscuit sounds like the ultimate treat for spoiling your pup. When shopping for cheese, make sure to avoid cheese types with additional herbs and spices. Go for the plain cheese, as this always works.

**Cooking time: 20 minutes**

**Yields: 12**

**Ingredients:**

- 3 Tablespoons coconut oil
- 2 cups old fashioned oats
- 1 cup cheddar cheese, shredded
- 2 Eggs

**Instructions:**

Preheat the oven to 350 degrees.

Add the old-fashioned oats to a blender and blend until you have a fine flour.

Add the rest of the treat ingredients and blend until combined.

Spread onto a flat, floured surface and cut out the shapes using a paw cookie cutter. Place onto a paper-lined baking sheet and bake for 15 to 20 minutes or until set.

# Special icing for dog cookies

When you want to add a bit of visual touch to your cookies, consider this recipe. It shows you how to prepare special icing adjusted for pups. Not only are the ingredients healthy, but it also makes the cookies look special.

**Cooking time: 10 minutes**

**Yields: ¾ cup**

**Ingredients:**

- 1/2 cup of plain yogurt
- 1/2 cup of Tapioca Starch
- 3 tsp. of milk
- food coloring of your choice, optional

**Instructions:**

Mix the tapioca starch and plain yogurt in a bowl until combined.

Add milk tablespoon at a time and mix until you reach the desired consistency.

Divide into smaller bowls and add food coloring of your choice if you want so.

Decorate your puppy cookies and let them enjoy the flavor.

# Heart shaped cookie sandwiches for pups

Cookie sandwiches are a great choice, but only when they are made of carefully chosen ingredients. These lovely cookies look so adorable and contain only approved ingredients to make your pup healthy.

**Cooking time:50 minutes**

**Yields:12**

**Ingredients:**

- 1/2 Cup Rolled Oats
- 2 cups Whole Wheat Flour
- 2 Large Eggs
- 1/2 Cup Peanut Butter
- 1 Cup Beet

*For the Icing:*

- 1/2 cup Greek Yogurt
- 3 Tablespoons of Water
- 1/2 cup Potato Starch

**Instructions:**

Preheat the oven to 375 degrees.

Chop the beets into chunks and add them to the food processor.

Add the eggs and blend until they get a pink color.

Add peanut butter, oats, and flour. Combine and remove the dough.

Knead the dough and add some more water if it is too dry.

Roll the dough and cut out the cookies with a cookie cutter.

Align them on a paper-lined baking sheet and bake for 20 minutes.

Mix the icing ingredients but add only two tablespoons of water. Add the remaining water little by little until you reach the desired consistency.

Allow the cookie to cool down and decorate them with the icing.

# Dog treats for fresh breath

Bad breath can be a significant difficulty for canines. This recipe solves this problem within a few steps. The treats contain secret ingredients that will improve their dental health.

**Cooking time:40 minutes**

**Yields:24**

**Ingredients:**

- 2 cups oat flour
- 1 egg
- ¼ cup fresh mint leaves
- ½ cup fresh parsley
- 2 tablespoon coconut oil
- 3 drops peppermint essential oil
- 2 tablespoon water

**Instructions:**

Preheat the oven to 350 degrees.

Line the baking pan with paper and set it aside.

Finely chop your herbs or place them in the food processor.

Combine all the dog treat ingredients except for the water. Mix well and knead the dough with your hands. Add water little by little if the dough is too dry.

Sprinkle oat flour on a flat surface and roll out the dough. Cut out the cookies and align them onto the baking sheet.

Bake for half an hour and remove once cooled down.

# Simple dog treats

We all understand that sometimes you don't have enough time for cooking. However, feel free to prepare a double batch of these treats and have them stored for later. This recipe is very easy to prepare. Let's try it!

**Cooking time:40 minutes**

**Yields:24**

**Ingredients:**

- 8 oz minced chicken breasts
- 2 egg yolks
- 1 Tablespoon Butter
- 4 carrots
- ½ cup flour

**Instructions:**

Preheat the oven to 340 degrees.

Process the carrots in a food blender until finely crushed.

Warm the butter and fry the carrots.

Transfer to a bowl and add the chicken and egg yolks.

Add flour and mix well. Add some more flour if the mixture is too sticky.

Shape in small sticks and bake for half an hour on a paper-lined sheet.

# Puppy donuts

If you thought that donuts aren't healthy, think twice. This recipe shows you how to make special donuts for puppies. Your dog will love it!

**Cooking time:30 minutes**

**Yields:6**

**Ingredients:**

- 1 cup Flour
- 1/2 Cup Peanut Butter
- 1/3 Cup Coconut Oil
- 1 Cup Oats
- 2 Eggs

*Topping:*

- 4 tablespoons Greek Yogurt
- 2 tablespoons Bacon Bits

**Instructions:**

Preheat the oven to 375 degrees.

Grease a donut pan and remove it aside.

Mix the ingredients in a bowl, except for the topping ingredients. Knead with your hands to combine the dough.

Place the dough into each compartment of the donut pan. Bake for 15 minutes or until set. Wait to cool before removing from the molds.

One cool, top with Greek yogurt and sprinkle bacon bits.

# Herbs dog treats

Herbs are excellent for your dog's dental health. This recipe shows you how to prepare tasty dog treats that will impress your best fur friend.

**Cooking time:** 30 minutes

**Yields:** 24

**Ingredients:**

- 4 cups whole wheat flour
- 1 egg
- 1 tbsp coconut oil
- 1/2 cup parsley, chopped
- 1 cup mint, chopped
- 1 cup water

**Instructions:**

Preheat the oven to 350 degrees.

Mix eggs, water, and coconut oil in a bowl.

Add the flour gradually and mix in between until you reach the right dog consistency.

Add the mint and parsley and incorporate them into the dough.

If it is too dry or too sticky, adjust with more water or flour.

Roll the dough into a floured surface. Use a paw or bone cookie cutter to shape the treats.

Align onto a paper-lined baking sheet. Bake for 15 minutes or until set.

# Pumpkin dog ice cream

Who said that dogs couldn't enjoy ice cream? This simple recipe shows you how to make dog ice cream and make your pup happy. They will definitely ask for more!

**Cooking time: 2 hours 20 minutes**

**Yields: 12**

**Ingredients:**

- 1/2 cup pumpkin puree, no additives
- 2 tbsp peanut butter
- 2 tbsp honey
- 32 oz plain whole milk yogurt

**Instructions:**

Warm the peanut butter and honey.

Mix them with the pumpkin puree until incorporated.

Add in the yogurt and combine.

Divide into cups and freeze for at least 2 hours.

# Bacon bites

Dogs love bacon, so don't skip on these lovely bacon bites. Don't forget that you can prepare a double batch for next time.

**Cooking time:1 hour**

**Yields:24**

**Ingredients:**

- 1 cup beef broth
- ½ cup powdered milk
- 1/3 cup bacon fat
- 1 egg, beaten
- 3 cups whole wheat flour

**Instructions:**

Preheat the oven to 325.

Add the broth to a pot and heat to medium heat. Add the bacon fat and stir until dissolved.

Add egg and powdered milk to the mixture.

Add one cup of flour and stir. Repeat until flour is gone.

Roll the bacon treat dough on a flat surface until half-inch thick.

Shape the cookies with the desired cookie cutter. Arrange a baking sheet with baking paper and align the treats.

Bake for 50 minutes or until set. Let them completely cool before serving.

# Puppy breath treats

Another useful recipe for bad breath. Munching on these amazing dog treats will improve their oral health. The crunchy texture and secret ingredients are the secrets that make it work.

**Cooking time:45 minutes**

**Yields:24**

**Ingredients:**

- 1 can chickpeas, drained and rinsed
- 1/2 cup fresh mint
- 1/2 cup fresh parsley
- 1 egg, large

**Instructions:**

Preheat the oven to 350.

Add all of the treat ingredients into a blender. Blend until thoroughly combined and smooth.

Transfer into silicone molds and bake for around 40 minutes or until set. Let the treats cool down before removing them from their molds.

# Blackberry cheesecake dog treats

Feed them with this amazing dessert and make them so happy. This recipe is also easy to prepare. Try it!

**Cooking time:30 minutes**

**Yields:12**

**Ingredients:**

- 1 egg
- 1/2 cup pureed blackberries
- 1/4 cup cream cheese, softened
- 1 tbsp ground flax seed
- 1 tbsp gelatin powder
- ½ teaspoon cinnamon
- 1 1/2 cups of brown rice flour

**Instructions:**

Preheat the oven to 350 degrees.

Mix the fruit puree, egg, cream cheese, cinnamon, gelatin, and flax.

Add the flour gradually while mixing. Work into a dough and add some more flour if it is too sticky.

Roll onto a flat surface sprinkled with flour. Create the treats with a cookie cutter.

Align on a paper-lined baking sheet and bake the treats for around 10 to 15 minutes or until dry.

# Puppy pancakes

This is a recipe that you can enjoy together with your puppy. Prepare a double act, one for you, one for your furry friend. Add blueberries or bananas as a topping for them. Enjoy!

**Cooking time:20 minutes**

**Yields:8**

**Ingredients:**

- 1 large egg
- 1 medium banana
- 2 tablespoons almond flour
- 2 tablespoons Coconut oil

**Instructions:**

Mash the banana with a fork.

Add flour and egg and mix with your hand mixer.

Heat your pan with coconut oil on medium.

Scoop some of the mixture and fry the pancakes for a minute or two or until light brown. Flip and repeat.

Let them cool completely and serve your dog.

# Conclusion

Now, when you have all of these wonderful dog recipes in your hands, you can start cooking. You will never have to hesitate about which ingredients to use or conduct in-depth research. This cookbook gathers only the best recipes with approved ingredients for dogs. Your puppies deserve to be loved and shown appreciation with some healthy home-cooked treats.

Whether you want to spoil them with cupcakes, pancakes, or homemade dog cookies, be sure that this cookbook will be your ultimate guide.

We hope that you enjoyed this fun and entertaining journey. Don't miss the other cookbooks from our collection!

# About the Author

Nancy Silverman is an accomplished chef from Essex, Vermont. Armed with her degree in Nutrition and Food Sciences from the University of Vermont, Nancy has excelled at creating e-books that contain healthy and delicious meals that anyone can make and everyone can enjoy. She improved her cooking skills at the New England Culinary Institute in Montpelier Vermont and she has been working at perfecting her culinary style since graduation. She claims that her life's work is always a work in progress and she only hopes to be an inspiration to aspiring chefs everywhere.

Her greatest joy is cooking in her modern kitchen with her family and creating inspiring and delicious meals. She often says that she has perfected her signature dishes based on her family's critique of each and every one.

Nancy has her own catering company and has also been fortunate enough to be head chef at some of Vermont's most exclusive restaurants. When a friend suggested she share some of her outstanding signature dishes, she decided to add cookbook author to her repertoire of personal achievements. Being a technological savvy woman, she felt the e-book realm would be a better fit and soon she had her first cookbook available online. As of today, Nancy has sold over 1,000 e-books and has shared her culinary experiences and brilliant recipes with people from all over the world! She plans on expanding into self-help books and dietary cookbooks, so stayed tuned!

# Author's Afterthoughts

Thank you for making the decision to invest in one of my cookbooks! I cherish all my readers and hope you find joy in preparing these meals as I have.

There are so many books available and I am truly grateful that you decided to buy this one and follow it from beginning to end.

I love hearing from my readers on what they thought of this book and any value they received from reading it. As a personal favor, I would appreciate any feedback you can give in the form of a review on Amazon and please be honest! This kind of support will help others make an informed choice on and will help me tremendously in producing the best quality books possible.

My most heartfelt thanks,

*Nancy Silverman*

*If you're interested in more of my books, be sure to follow my author page on Amazon (can be found on the link Bellow) or scan the QR-Code.*

*https://www.amazon.com/author/nancy-silverman*

www.ingramcontent.com/pod-product-compliance
Lightning Source LLC
Chambersburg PA
CBHW062209270325
24228CB00031B/677